COOS RIVER
REVERBERATIONS

COOS RIVER REVERBERATIONS

POEMS OF RIVER, FARM & FOREST

GUY CRAIG

THOUGHTS ON THE GOOD LIFE PRESS
Oregon, USA

COOS RIVER REVERBERATIONS:

POEMS of RIVER, FARM & FOREST

Published by

THOUGHTS ON THE GOOD LIFE PRESS

Portland, Oregon

www.ThoughtsOnTheGoodLife.com

© Copyright 2021 by GUY CRAIG

Written by GUY CRAIG

Artwork and Cover Design by SARAH CRAIG

For inquires, write to the author, with the subject line "Inquires," at the email address below.

Hello@ThoughtsOnTheGoodLife.com

Visit - GuyCraigPoetry.com

This book is a work of fiction. Names, characters, places, and incidents either are the product of the author's imagination or are used fictitiously, and any resemblance to actual persons, living or dead, events, organizations, or locales is entirely coincidental.

ISBN: 978-1-7334968-2-7

For my wife Sarah and my son Kenneth,
and my parents Lorenzo and Laura Craig.

With gratitude to my great-grandparents
from the Coos River Valley:
Lorenzo A. and Stella Justrom Cutlip.

And deep appreciation and love for my
family and friends.

If you think dear reader,
by these few words
I might (in some way) mean you,
then, of course, you must now know—
it has always been so,
yet never more true.

CONTENTS

Introduction x

POEMS

Setting I: River

On the River We Float 4
Tidal River Swimming Hole 6
Contrary Bend 7
Birth of the Coos River Beauty Apple 8
Down by the Creek 11
Coos River School 13
Rope Swing Tryst 15
We Talk to the River 17
Coos River Cemetery 19
Mr. Buzzard 22
Night Swimming 25
Stars 27
Community of Idlewood 29

CONTENTS

Setting II: Farm

A Walk in the Fields 33
Looking Out the Classroom Window 35
Afternoon Music Hour 39
A Summer Home 41
Riverside Garden Work Party 43
Homemade Smoker 46
Salmon on the Fire Pit 48
Taking Care 50
Gone Too Soon 51
Barbed Wire 54
River Field Burn Pile 57
Outworked 59
Late Fall Work in the Fields 61
The Wind Storm 65
Grandfather's Study 67
Blue Smoke Around the Card Table 77
Shared Well 79
Cow Jam 80
Firewood Row 85
Short Rib 87
Himalayan Blackberry 89
Summer Hammocks 91
Woodstove in the Old Ranch House 94
To Town 96

CONTENTS

Setting III: Forest

Through the Canyon to the Clearing 101
A Walk up the Draw to Recharge 105
Endless Ferns 108
When I Grow Up 110
Myrtle Nuts 115
Skunk Cabbage 118
Chittum Bark 121
Maple Leaves Piled in the Dry Creek Bed 123
Myrtle Grove 125
Rancher and a Logger 129
Living Near the Stream 133
Froze Last Night 135
Dusk 137

Acknowledgments 139
Afterword 142
Suggestions for Further Reading 143

COOS RIVER
REVERBERATIONS

Introduction

In many ways, the poems in this collection are an ode to the people and place of the Coos River Valley, near Coos Bay, Oregon. The fifty poems have been inspired by my thoughts and experiences, the excellent historical texts on the area, and my Swedish-Finn ancestors who first moved to the Coos River Valley in the late 19th century.

My favorite historical text on the Coos River Valley, and the one which I believe complements these poems the best is: *Coos River Echoes: A Story of the Coos River Valley*, by Charlotte L. Mahaffy, published in 1965, who made the valuable observation in her book introduction:

"Where the stream was the main highway for decades . . . the ingress into the valley being by boat made for a way of life unique in itself."

I have always considered *Coos River Echoes* integral to appreciating and understanding this region's culture and people, a history written with a tremendous amount of heart and a spirit that makes the book akin to a poem.

U.S. poet laureate, Billy Collins, said in a Washington Post article:[*]

"Poetry is the only history we have of human emotions. Most history books, what we call history books, are stories of battles and treaties, negotiations and beheadings and coronations. But poetry is the only reminder of this very essential part of being human, which is one's emotional life and all the dimensions it entails."

I hope these poems build upon the rich history of human emotion of the Coos River Valley, in particular, and more generally, any river valley; may they convey a sense of "home" (life's vicissitudes and all) and "this place was made for you."

Warmly,

Guy Craig

---

*Lillian Cunningham, "Billy Collins on Life, Death and Poetry," The Washington Post, April 23, 2019, accessed January 28, 2021, https://www.washingtonpost.com/news/on-leadership/wp/2014/10/03/billy-collins-on-life-death-and-poetry/)

SETTING I
RIVER

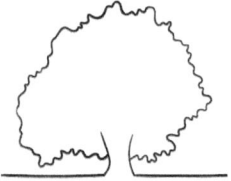

*Shimmer afar as my chair
sinks in the sandbar,
a sudden loud splash,
a squeal and a crash
cover the sound
of the ice rattling in my drink jar.*

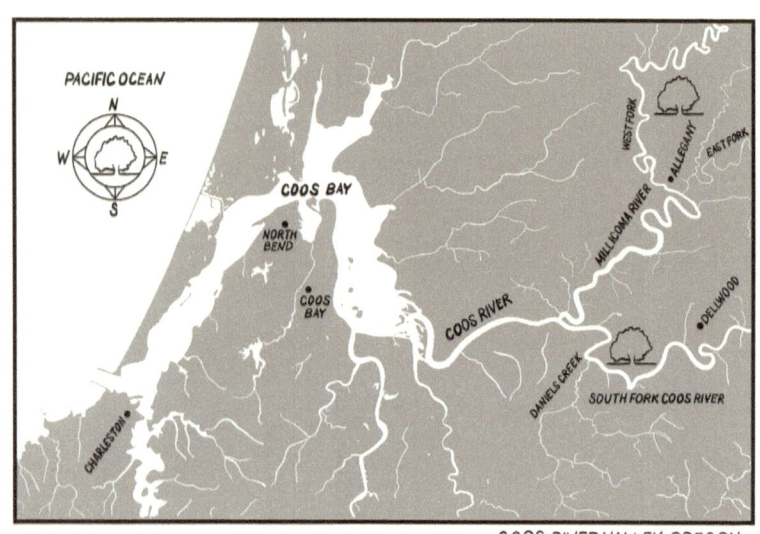

COOS RIVER VALLEY, OREGON

On the River We Float

I am upriver without care,
free of town's weight and structure,
as my untempered soul and bent frame
the cool-summer water gently laps,
this partial shade from the shore's willow and myrtle
a welcome, freckled cap, signaling celebration—
like finding the sum goods of all the drawn Xs
on all the world's real treasure maps.

Returned to this once ocean island chain of clearing water—
my spirit swimming, like varied fish in a stream—
staying in motion as day turns to night, my blood memory,
a keeper of history, in my body's own way.

Deep currents, like knowledge—
a pressing measure of time,
when not here, often wondering
if I have enough energy beyond surviving,
the world is not always kind.

But, hope, like this river, has tied me to you,
in a world where I might see you playing lightly
on the tide-forged river hewn, out with steady
and cherished friends—like me, this summer,
where once again, my soul mends;

so timely and unfaded,
life this year has been so askew.

Why can't I live this way always?

Over the years, I have often wondered:

Can I be made quite whole, by the run to this goal?

Or, will my good luck run its course—
no room here for big life mistakes (no gold here)
if unprepared—King Midas of gorse?

When I was much younger,
no great and happy believer in fate,
now more west-traveled and older,
fewer right paths before nature's gate—

today, I finally see clearly—

this place was made for me.

Tidal River Swimming Hole

Foam circles on top,
leaves drifting below,
back this way
in ten minutes or so.

No need to hurry,
let me commune
on this incoming tide
with no slack till noon.

Slow circle now,
I am spinning round,
just a few more loops
before heading to town?

Might as well tarry
with the afternoon breeze,
with the sea salt ions
through the grass and the leaves—

life repeats,
and it can soothe,
this time is for me,
my nature's truth.

Contrary Bend

Becalmed, again, old friend,
on apt named Contrary Bend;
never a less likely place
for a sail to rend.

Some wind is here,
I know it;
though this sheltered bit of land
does not care now to bestow it.

All paths on land or water,
have their peculiar airs;
this one too asks only you see
through her shimmering, yet still, portieres.

So, when you find that shy wind,
be ready to trim the sails,
for a time will come,
we will go faster than free summer ales.

Birth of the Coos River Beauty Apple

Land below,
below;
land for grant,
for plant.

Dew above,
above;
dew is right,
in light.

Buy below,
below;
buy to stow,
to grow.

Scion above,
above;
scion for wrap,
for tap.

Graft below,
below;
graft for stash,
for cash.

Grow above,
above;
grow in ground,
in mound.

Tend below,
below;
tend to care,
to care.

Harvest above,
above;
harvest is late,
is fate.

Travel below,
below;
travel is long,
be strong.

Dry above,
above;
dry to store,
for more.

Sail below,
below;
sail to bay,
to convey.

Sale above,
above;
sale for health,
for wealth.

Sleep below,
below;
sleep at river,
a shiver.

Legacy above,
above;
legacy in-store,
in lore.

Down by the Creek

When I was young,
I would often seek
to swim in the Daniels Creek,

with nothing enjoyed more
then to catch trout for dinner
or ferrying-shaped tree limbs, stout and en route
to splash the cares of heat from the workday.

Wholly inviting it was to early escape
from the chore of putting in the hay.

It was such a treat of earned relief
to fall, bare feet first, through the hot mire,

sweeping below the summer-cold, water ripple
to the refreshing short-timed hold of renewal.

Generous family and neighborly,
fun-loving friends of place and spirit,

were inclined to spend time with kids
of all relations and mixed degrees of kin

who were full of the need
for endless adventures,
and prone to flip their lids.

Names on family pictures are fading,
like my memories,
since I more than waded in that fine creek,

and I think I would feel more complete,
and life might rarely ever feel tepid or bleak,
if I spent more time immersed in those healing waters.

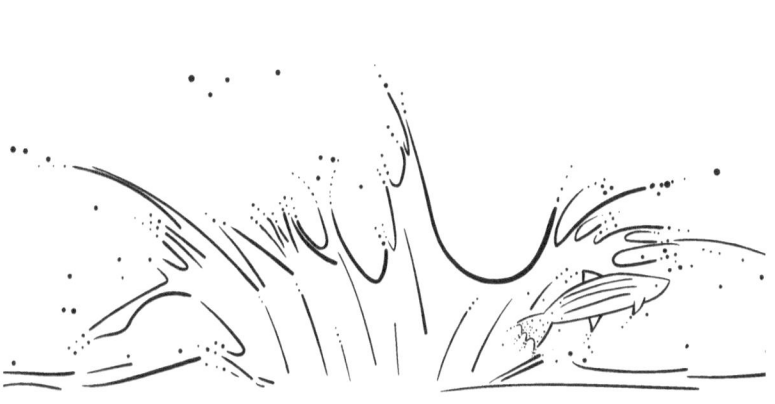

Coos River School

Time went so exceedingly fast;
each memory—a flashcard,
too early recess whistle,
or how soon I missed the sounds
of rustling in the hallway
from the hanging up of coats
and the putting away of backpacks
after silently leaving the classroom that last time.

I attended through 2nd grade,
metaphorically felled, like you, by ballot measure;
after you closed, another school won the bid,
yet fond memories I still have of you—

Halloween haunted houses,
not only in the gym but the school within,
with bobbing apples, scarecrows,
long-winding and decorated cardboard trick tunnels,
smiling teachers, staff, and volunteers
brought joy and great laughs.

A place to trick or treat,
with costumes on display,
pumpkins as well as hay;

a time for just good, clean, country fun—
oh, what a long time did you run.

Like the past, long gone, of travel to school
by riverboats, horses, and game trails,
you are no more, but like the original school
built there before you,
you kept at your core, caring for the people.

A church now in your place,
with indoor and outdoor stands,
and seems in good hands,
from diplomas conferred,
presently to weddings, food drives,
and soul attending, all currently preferred.

With the power of place at your core,
your spirit which has lasted long,
seems to have the best chance to prolong
our sense of community,
if caring before can be any prediction
of a caring future.

Rope Swing Tryst

Myrtles have the fewest hurdles,
so Kraken armed, with gnarly curdles
to fly unwinding and quickly
from tight, large spun rope,
an airborne, whirling-eddy spirit,
present and alive with great hope.

—All summer long,
I have improved my swing,
and now I will try
my high rope circus fling,
while swinging, I'll climb up one rung higher—
I have really thought it through,
all will admire.

—Off I go,
I am quickly spinning round,
right arm let go,
unforeseen gravity profound;

only one arm was to go,
but now it is two—
oh!—I am falling,
what should I do?

*—That barbed wire river fence below
looks like my fateful target,
never so close to it even if I charged it—
landing on my left wrist,
now rolling stop;
this wooden fence post,
a scary block.*

*—Out of breath, and wrist seems loose,
run to mom for ice to reduce,
then head off to town
to mend my left broken wrist—*

*perhaps it is time to end this
youthful rope swing tryst.*

We Talk to the River

I have a fine-banked place
to release my pain,
on that river shore,
I think gone loved ones reflect the same—

with my good vision obscured
with rain like tears,
I sense strong memories
let them know my fears.

Why do some others often come here too?
For sure, it is not planned—
so strange, nature's pull communes
with us near where we land.

Your favorite beer,
I pour it out,
the bubbles float down your old boat route,
somehow this helps me to remember you;

you smile big and wide,
and a laugh escapes free,
this helps me breathe again,
and your comfort's warmth elates me.

Now that I am away,
I stop by less often than in the past,
since sometimes life gets busy
(the one thing in this life I can do without),

but I am hopeful now in a way
I have not been since before you were gone,
my tide is rising again in a thinning fog;

I may not be alright since I am still healing,
but I am no longer feeling empty,
nor worried my life purpose is still unmet,
or my approach to discovery so wrong.

Coos River Cemetery

A home with a river view,
settlers more than a few,
may I settle there the same
when my time is due.

What stories they would tell,
up in the Dellwood, or Allegany,
about the Coos River Valley below—

likely, more material for *Coos River Echoes*
of varied and full lives,
precious stories of long classics and short fads
full of dances, weddings, funerals,
summer home meals, clubs,
and, so tearfully too, early deaths
of some of their cherished lasses and lads.

A river as a road is not always safe
when lost in the creek,
or drowned by the river,
ponds, or swamp lakes.

So many sad tales mixed in with the good,
but carry on most did,

since they knew better than to early grave dig,
if nothing but for the sake
that a dutiful life is not a mistake.

They modeled taking the good with the bad,
knowing a life of significant enough length
no matter how glad,
it, too, will run over at times
with despair and remiss.

It seems none of us
know why we live this fate,
so I guess like them,
I am history bound
at nature's matriculating gait.

Learning about these people,
at least I can wonder and relate
to the knowledge that life is always
illusive, and since we few here
cannot peer beyond death,
conceivably that is not by chance or mistake.

So, like them, I will honor the day
by trusting I will find this once child's
time-lost peace and love
on the other side of a well-traveled journey.

On that silent cemetery overlook,
I will take comfort
that others have passed this way,
and they may someday welcome me home
with a good loved one's smile
and a joyous, well-earned stay.

Mr. Buzzard

Mr. Buzzaaard, you wily turkey vulture—
my old friend—as I look up,
right now to me, you are summer,
and even more so
when I was much younger.

In my youth, your flight did so please,
yet now older, you have become more offending—
a sort of death-pending breeze.

Up high in the air,
you float above the land and the seas,
up high in the air,
you selfishly glide mote-timed
for those on death's knees.

Still, you are a signal of my freedom
to run without shoes,
a pendulum of the seasons,
alive you pronounce,
confirm, and strangely bemuse.

Down along the river,
a long search, a short cruise—

no animal wasted,
no food too abused.

You seem to enjoy to fly in a circle
with your weathered traveling friends,
when not squaring off
with too many other vultures,
always testing your lens.

You have a careful, long look,
you try to avoid trouble,
easier for you
with the mimicking death shuffle?

And, not even in your youth,
do you appear as fresh as others in suckle—
the older I get, the less harmless you appear—

a harbinger of death,
after all the summers dear;
my time now so much shorter,
my options more clear.

But, welcome back again, old friend—
I am still alive as you can see—

though seeing your wing's shadow today,
was harder on me.

It still made me straighten (though sorely)
with an almost skip to my step,
and I suddenly wondered, almost wistfully,
how many seasons of reasons I have left.

Now, fortunately, once again back to my better instincts,
and with you safely moored in my stable sight,
my young joy is returning an answer
from the resounding call to the healing summer season—

oh, and today was *so* full of great,
late morning blue sky song,
inviting me to slowly fall forward
through time and embrace every last bit of this echoing,

life-enhancing, sandstone-colored setting sun,
whose reflective heat keeps me reverberantly inspired,
freely moving around each year,

wherever you and I can lovingly belong.

Night Swimming

Sudden summer night swimming,
means good times are brimming,
the star wind can be cool,
but this river is warm like an old thermal pool.

Generally, a sandbar or dock
will support the echo
of gleeful splash shock.

But, underappreciated
in my personal view,
is the lack of water animals
who see me as chew.

Like all forested areas
one still must show care,
but few places in the world,
during summer seem so safe—
gratefully, the danger so rare.

No poisonous snakes
to swim with me,
nor below the water,
dangers from critters brew.

So, tonight I will swim free
from the willow hugged riverbank,
in this small, open clearing
to wash the new-chanced sand
from between my safe toes.

With a fast, out-of-the-gate, running dive,
Doppler effect in full stride,
I will announce my arrival,

then after a leisurely and joyful stay,
I will let the full blue moon
lighthouse my way back
to the welcoming shore.

Stars

Away from town,
as the light goes to ground
I like to sit and quietly watch
the brightening stars.

The flap of an owl,
a far off strange small growl
the air moves across
my relaxed, careworn, old face.

The air I breathe in,
and my chest does ascend,
as my head and my eyes
move slightly tipped back.

Shimmer afar as my chair
sinks in the sandbar,
a sudden loud splash,
a squeal and a crash
cover the sound
of the ice rattling in my drink jar.

The night is alive with the chase,
our world is spinning on pace,
I find watching stars does imbue

the glory of the universe in view,
I am so lucky tonight
lets me life-hew.

Community of Idlewood

Paradise, this South Fork river,
the garden valley full deliver,
with your first name sent bay-bound to history
like a steam-powered, tugboat pulled log raft,
1940 postal officials found Idlewood
too similar to the town of Idlelyd, of the next county,
so a new, welcoming name was made to craft.

Little homes, where are you now?
No steamboat mate to wave from the bow.
You, once the setting of freshet-driven splash dams
and named before large, local sawmill nixing—
full of hillside gardens, hunting, and future fish fixing.

For a time, you had a mighty lodge,
now come and gone, like Orvile Dodge.

Route by riverboat
on *Alice H., Welcome, Rainbow, and Favorite*,
milk cans, school children, city folks for picnics,
and grateful neighbors did savor it.

Dellwood now, you carry on,
a fading picture of one more dawn.

SETTING II
FARM

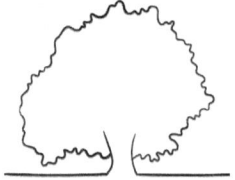

*A garden valley we are in—
cloistered, salty bay breezed, wild flowered,
with surprisingly myrtle scented bees.*

A Walk in the Fields

Never so healed
as after a walk in the fields—
many a stroll I have indulged.

And, never a sign I was wasting time—
we do not have all the answers to this world.

I like to consider that if I had a past life,
I was the highest bidder,
or I could not be good enough,
so I was just lucky.

Maybe my last road
was not so easily hoed—
so this life—a present to live.

I am never so glad
as when a walk can be had
alone or with family and friends.

Not all are so lucky to have such,
in this world, so lovely a crutch.

And, almost nothing in life I would rather do,

so if you cannot reach me,
know at least, if walking in the fields,
I am where I should be,
and you can be too.

Looking Out the Classroom Window

In the fall, while in high school,
I would often look out the classroom window
at nature, the jewel, and I was obsessed.

Why was I going to practice again
on another sunny afternoon?

These training structures
after a long day of class,
energizing for some, but draining for me.

I suppose I have always been called to the land,
maybe not an unexpected attachment
for a happy, freedom-loving youth
who grew up next to what seemed
like a privately discovered,
boundaryless, coastal mountain.

I lived like an enterprising tinkerer,
and I seldom got bored,
yet for a competitive,
small-town youth,
testing myself against peers

was also always a calling so strong that
I chose to restrain my secure love of nature
to better help overcome my insecure sense of self.

And, for most of my life
that has been the dynamic,
but now that I am older,
the quieter voice to spend more time in nature
is almost the only voice I wish to hear,
and it keeps getting louder—
beckoning me home.

Today, when I reflect,
I get taken away to a time
and place of such peace
where I am always out in the air,
blissfully light and warmed,
insulated from the carried weight
and the winters of life.

I know my place in the world,
and that knowledge gives me such faith,
that access to nature's beauty and comfort
heal through and outside of all time.

Now, often away,
my shared words with you,
are my heart's echo
of a magical time and place.

And the hope I feel—
though not always constant—
when home near the river,

is like an unexpectedly hiked upon
wild cherry blossom display
of abundance—

full of numerous,
almost uncountable blossoms,
yet somehow, the world never runs out of room
and the land is nurtured each passing day
by every bloom.

Afternoon Music Hour

When Grandfather retired,
much music he sired,
making my early afternoons
so full of good sound.

In summer, double front doors wide open—
piano notes floating breezily away as softly
as colorful, rhododendron flower scents.

A few songs in the queue,
ones he loved,
minded and renewed.

The music, a centerline through his life,
and I suppose now mine, as I reflect
how confident I feel when I am settled and still
as the notes help me keep a good temperament
and a more harmonious path.

This stringed life near the river, a siren to me—
playing light and secure—
this timing brings me back to full joy
and the life I have procured.

I am reminded in this present
moment that my life is
always enhanced and soothed
through these sounds,

so on this orienting afternoon,
may I also be a tuned comfort
to my leisurely guests
and dear listening friends.

A Summer Home

No place quite so sweet,
as the summer river home, you can keep,
though harder to find for most,
and an expensive way to host.

But, by work of the brow,
or inheritance trowel
the result is one and the same—

the place must be alight
with supernal sights which delight
all the senses to take heavy cares away.

So, a sensible place to start
is with flower seeds thrown in an arc
while remembering to get those bulbs planted in the fall.

A few wildflower volunteers,
can add to the cheer
on half an acre as course,
which will only add to the source of splendor,
mirth, and contentment that abounds.

One must also take care
to remember to share,
for the wise always say
that a life of abundance
is enhanced by what good we best can give.

Not the paths to the absence of pain,
nor care to often find financial gain
(though nice) is really doing (that) much.

So, plant some bright flowering shrubs
and native, fragrant fruit trees,
for such an idyllic scene
to lift the weight of the world
from your welcome guests
as well as help you live out a long summer
of harvestable joy, leisure, and plentiful rest.

Riverside Garden Work Party

Tilled with heavy, sweating brow,
forty yards long by ten yards wide,
I hope we have enough energy when done
to sow the crisscross pattern in line.

The sandy old pine soil tastes bittersweet,
the rototiller has made it
all barrel-waved rows and ecstatically neat.

So tempting for the deer, this future resplendent,
fresh and crunchy contained treat,

that we must now just build the deer fence,
and not feel bad that out nature's gate,
such a bundled cornucopia
they never would meet.

This garden will bring
canning and dry store planning
to be added to our smoking and broaching,
which means that friends and family
will more likely have something ripe
through abundant planting,
not unfortunate poaching.

A garden valley we are in—
cloistered, salty bay breezed, wild flowered,
with surprisingly myrtle scented bees.

After work, sweat-laden and dry soil coated,
we will shake off the dust of dried clay
and pull a cold beer out of the fridge
or a neat, olive-stirred "nifter" off the tray.

We will get ready to eat some of last year's
harvest of the day, and share some irreverent laughs
and good chatter as we recount the refreshing,
yet odorous and cooling wind off the river—
blown from the bi-monthly, minus tide,
heavily impacted Coos Bay.

When dinner is ready
and all is put away,
our energy lagging
and hearts full of play,
talking may lull,
but let our love never sway.

Homemade Smoker

From cedar siding built strong,
four feet wide, by three feet deep,
by six feet high, a smokehouse was built.

Inside, six sturdy metal racks
all laid level and straight,
and fed by a dirt-covered tunnel,
metal barrel cut lengthwise as a fire plate.

Many fighting shad were hit by smoke,
bones so soft not to choke—
oh, such harvesting fun did the fish provoke,
even more fun to catch than smallmouth bass per stroke,

if not in every heavy sounding strike on the fishing pole,
then each potent early-summer flash of memory
of the reaffirming river churning from abundant schooling,
past the ready, fishing boats and the sturdy, welcoming dock—

paired with frothy, boisterous, and occasionally tipsy,
long echoing friendship toasts of times past,
sometimes forgotten in this busy world,
but loved by many, again recorded, and preserved to last.

Spring and fall Chinook salmon too,
were brought through the long smoke
while courses of striped bass
(for a few years) came through en masse.

As we opened the door,
smoke would waft from ceiling to floor
causing a choking, big watering-eyed step back,

and we would look giddily
at all the fish on each rack—
fish scales all removed,
the skin stuck and improved
was now nature's perfect raft
and so ready to graft
before taking it back to the house;

great care was always taken
not to overconsume on the first swoon.

The pantry was always ensured to have space,
for the joy of seeing a wall of canned jars
in winter, is a kind of warmth and grace
experienced most finely by the grateful—
in a well-stocked and run place.

Salmon on the Fire Pit

What can be better than to sit by the fire,
with a circle of chairs to retire and admire,
of course, using one's own chair sitting alone
can be a good thing to do,
but better it seems to view with a crew.

Sandstones all around
to gravel the ground,
a fire pit made
for this place to astound.

In late fall and in the early spring,
fillet salmon I was happy to bring—

open with care,
to prepare for good fare
of parsley, garlic,
and lemon on a bed of butter
with a steady sear of the meat,
then skin side until neat—
barbequed thirty-five
to forty-five minutes over hot coals.

As a child, I ate so much salmon it would seem,
that not until I was five in dog years was I again keen.

Yet, the unapologetic fun we did have
and the good memories we did calve,
with an empty plate, dark and late,
we made sure to stare at the stars and our fate.

Taking Care

With my parents, I had to take care,
since even while I was still learning to write, I sensed then,
as humbleness as an adult, allows me to understand now,
their young love for their children
was still luckily spirited and present—

not yet resigned,
like too many pen-written essential items on a checklist,
nor exhausted, like a quick game,
turned unending, of revolving chairs,
where you really win by escaping to the next room.

My parents knew of all the dangers
for a child like me in this world,
so they used words to catch and protect me,
woven ever so carefully, like a river weir
to help me be aware of false paths
and learn to hew a new approach.

How often I laughed and discounted,
the questions and the thoughts feared,
since I was gifted and invincible,
my world happily surmounted.

But, truth there was in what my parents would say,
too many times, I frivolously risked without benefit
a much too early end, and for them, some sad, tired days.

Gone Too Soon

I feel your pressed hand upon my shoulder,
I don't have you, yet I must get older
since you have left this land, I must be bolder.

What am I to do with my new child, and my new life?
Twenty years more we thought we had of you,
my valued father gone, at just the eve of our end strife.

The room is quiet, weight sinking, feel blue—
can anything here ever lift my bleak review?

We fought, we talked, you guided me through,

but I still had so many vital questions to ask—
so many stories to hear of your past
(I was still young), our time did not last.

Older now . . . even than you,
would you be proud
of what I have made it through?

I raised that child,
and my love and I
helped care for others too.

I am still tempestuous
from time to time,
it must be hardwired,

and I think, tied to a high tolerance of pain—
so, I like to believe it helped
as a genetic, loving, keep-on-living gift,
I carry from you.

I wonder now,
what unfinished business
you felt you had left,
dying in your late fifties,
a life for some, just over half met;

while my own race is further along,
there are always some things left to do,
I suppose fewer now,
but I am older than once were you.

I like to think you were as content then
as I am now,
and I am so happy to know I was wrong
when I thought our time would not last,

since love, rich memories, and discovered stories
kept you alive somehow and helped me hold to you,
not just staying in the past,
but moving both steadily forward
and caringly through.

Barbed Wire

Old leather gloves
and wound metal of barbed wire,
dry my sweating hands
from nicks and new scars' ire,

so let this western red cedar
strong cross brace girdle
after I wind this last stick of myrtle.

Some wonder why I often rework
this unemployed fence,
I have no cattle now,
but this is the only way life makes sense.

Get me out early,
see my rising warm breath,
pour from my thermos—
I will take care of the rest.

Four more braces to build,
one more log to peel—
I have got old leather gloves
and wound barbed metal to feel.

I may complete the fences quickly
or take all year,
if they do not work as well as I planned,
I will tear them down and move them,
but I will still keep them in my sphere.

I need to keep moving to run far away
from disappointed thoughts
of regret, remorse, and delay;
sometimes, I work headlong for a sense of control
with a desire to share beauty and order.

I work this old unprofitable farmland
to help my family, friends, and neighbors
to feel that so far out here, we can still somehow
make it stay maintained,
improved, efficient, and conformed.

But, this land always grows
and tends to confound,
so it challenges
and makes my past work omissions,
lack of time, or money redound.

So, I will wake up tomorrow,
and I will most likely rework
another unemployed fence—
I have no cattle now,
but this is the only way life makes sense.

River Field Burn Piles

A crackling pile of wet tree limbs, leaves, and debris,
a contradictory scene you will not often see,
since burning in the rain and the cold
takes peculiar engineering of ignition,
those few who have tried it fully understand—
with porous nature, you have to be bold.

Once it gets going, truly lovely to see,
glowing and knowing only ash left will be,
especially looking at the center circle
of gray on the ground—
the red edge of flame in the pouring rain
will be expected but also confound.

Great plumes of grey and white smoke
may cause a few tears and even a choke,
since to get it all burned
you may need to stay in place
with hard brush cutting, measured pulling,
and thoughtful throwing to keep up with the pace.

But, *oh*, what a feeling
when the pile above is all gone—
ashes will wet smolder below
from here to a month or more dawns.

Outworked

I always thought myself of care,
so hard work I ventured,
without much despair,

yet never in all my days,
was I able to keep up
with my father's work ways.

On the day you know you are strong,
imagine if you kept that feeling lifelong
with each job a challenge to test your might,
each work party task
a sort of melee night fight.

As an adult, I marvel still
at fence posts dug in degrees of thrill
and trucks of firewood filled double strokes,
left throw, now right—hurry now, let's go!

Who needs sports,
when living with work so grand?

For me, all the following events
have seemed all too pretentious and canned.

You have to be adept to play against nature
the chance player as well the stage—
who competes with calculated gait
the long, great game of health against age.

When we tire,
or our attention is strained,
it slowly takes our victories
and laughs heartily at all our gains.

So, I will remember the extreme work
put out on the many days,
appreciate the many trials,

and wish hospitably others who might come late
to take over what has been our ways—
may they enjoy the game,

all the wins and all the play—
given they do not
ignorantly flout or discount
the hard-earned accomplishments
of my father's work ways.

Late Fall Work in the Fields

Strong, weathered hands caked heavy,
my fingernails cold and dried out;
clay, sand, loam, and rock,
spread on the ground in a muddy lost rout.

Deep in this revisited ditch,
my boots chunkily waterlogged
and sunk deep,
with this shovel heaver
of both narrow trench and shallow heap.

July, of course, would have clearly been best,
another delayed project, so like the rest,
but this cold rain comes,
heavy, piercing, and brisk—
must hurry now, before the day is long.

One-hundred years since many of these clay drainage
pipes were laid in the ground—
I hope this new culvert will last as long,
be as strong, and every bit as sound.

Professional farmers all in the past,
what have hobbyist farmers like myself
done so well to make it last?

The fact I even have and enjoy it, with my love
and children, has to be a great gift returned to my kin.

Yet, will I be the last to own it?

It seems I am the last to grow up here all year,
so will that change how my children
feel about the land, and will they feel
wholly so bound and endeared?

The land has a title of ownership—
the legal description of the place—
which can have great monetary value,
and be a safe keeper
of wealth and good taste.

But, that is only the start,
since for me,
it also most keenly mechanically wraps
memories through the embrace
of sound, sight, taste, smell, and touch—
the land, like any tool,
an extension of self.

How many years do we have left
to be present, healthy, and in command?

What will the family lose
of ourselves if we let go of the land?

But, memories and material legacy,
no matter how important,
also share the world with each generations' gifts,
potential, future, good and bad fortune.

So, I will endeavor
to not only rule from the past,
I will watch my children grow,
support their gifts,

share time with them on the land,
and once they are adults
we will each year check-in on our paths.

We will answer a question
to help avoid hurt from surprise—

will this land still be with us next year

or will it be another family's

love and fair new prize?

The Wind Storm

Candles set out,
racing-like wind song
moves fluidly and stout.

A raking alongside the house,
and only strong branches will sojourn
before finding company in creeks and puddles
also adorned with leaves,

mud, and long-past sticks,
as the gusty whooshing comes,
swirling heavily tonight, then it runs.

How much can these windows bear?

That tree too near, why did I not shear?

Oh, that broken treetop on the far hill,
almost had its own will.

Warm in the house now,
maybe take my bow,
I think, early to bed for me.

When the power goes,
better to be in bed with comfy toes;
perchance not a better place to enjoy
an old fashioned
woodstove low-glow night,
all the world will seem right.

Frozen pipes are a fright,
so, the faucet is not tight,
but a fire I will want built—
better tonight, a morning with no guilt.

The extra water jugs are now full,
the tea pot on the wood stove
should help calm tomorrow's lull.

Tired now, a melodic yawn,
sleep I enter until the dawn.

Grandfather's Study

From the fine bound and varied colored
hard-to-read books in Grandfather's study,
I eventually learned:

A path is open to those who wander
through winding ways and winds of sunder.

Friendly calls of time elapsed
have left fair lights as books and maps.

Attention to forms, goods, habit, and fortune
humble the mind and perfect devotion.

As a child, these always happily beckoning
yet fatiguing to comprehend and decipher
tomes and talismans of knowledge
challenged and inspired
whereas as an adult, these books seem
to now more often measure and expire
some of the hopes,
dreams, and visions of my youth.

Which, with time, has made me see
that it is ok to be glad that some futures
are not entirely meant to be.

Often late in the afternoon,
after school, I would venture down
to an overgrown,
old brick pit made imagined auditorium,

so thick with pine needle floors
and surrounded by Douglas fir,
sword fern, dogwood, salmonberry,

willow, and myrtle, where I would
give my political speeches
to my natural crowd of supporters.

I would give a mighty stump speech,
my voice aiming to carry one-hundred feet,
yet never so smooth
as to please both the unvoted firs and ferns,

I often provoked them
to make technical miscalculations
and planted the seeds for next election concerns.

When not an aspiring politician,
I was of a more retiring nature,
focused on a child's royal estate—

leisure-work and recreation through fort building
and maintaining, fishing, hunting, swimming,
map making, entertaining, reading history's great books,
watching movies, imagining, and good-natured delaying.

Such a precious and delicate space
when a child can dream without limits—
as they wrestle with the difference between
temperance and fortitude—
while wise adults listen with *some*
enjoyment, support, and curiosity—
often, a sign of life's hard-earned grace.

As I got older, I pursued my wonder about
both political service and the power of place.
No surprise, I suppose, having grown up on a tree farm,
with family lands all around, secured through the generations,

as well as many long-passed and a few alive
family members of once state representatives,
port commissioners, campaign managers, strategists,
political hobbyists, and three-term mayors.

For me, I wanted nothing more
then to be ready to serve,

if needed, in government service or politics—
nothing more than to follow
the heart-hewed steps of family leaders.

But, I was insight's, poor cousin,
and not naturally gifted or inclined
to use attention or power well,
often hurriedly dodging structured learning,
and any mature advice less than about 2,000 years old—
young and full of hubris, not yet knowing theory from praxis—
the common fate of radicals, unhinged idealists,
the proud unlearned, and the powerful who never doubt.

My grandfather often said:

—*Leaders have followers, if you have the ambition*;

I thought I did, but I led poorly—
often seeking prestige, power, intrigue, and fame
(too focused on using the tricks of attraction)
while responding to others, sometimes,
with apathy born of failures, anger out of fears,
and undisciplined control—forgetting or disregarding
tested ideals, the benevolence of norms,
and rules for heart and home.

A long-serving generational family of politicians,
firmly dedicated to constituents,
yet waning in political relevance,
can be an exceedingly hard place to learn
to serve each other kindly,

and a place sometimes filled
with blame, subtle discounting jests,
gossip, demanding expectations,
misdirection, and at times,
exacerbated and escaped contempt;

yet selfishly, I chose to continue
to try and lead others,
but the goods were only apparent,

so I offered little of real value,
not yet knowing my strengths,
and I found that I was not needed.

Maybe deservedly so, since even I knew then

that being charming in the wrong way often only offends;

incredibly, somehow, it seems upon reflection,
I have always been lucky to be open to ideas,
my saving grace, and this child of the idyllic countryside
also finally heard my grandfather say:

—There is no more beautiful place on earth
than here to enjoy, care for and learn about
ourselves, others, and the land.

A long-serving generational family of landowners
waxing in commitment to stewardship
can be a very magical place
to learn to serve each other kindly
through weekends and holidays together—

on the land, with music, work parties
for firewood cutting and stacking,
yard maintenance, home repairs,
boating, playing instruments,

teaching children about aesthetics,
and generously enjoying
and sharing gifts and the most meaningful events.

Now, older and more humble,
full of a bit more courage to create,
and a desire to be more faithful to self,
I can venture from politics and people
to people and place, wishing those on the first path well,
understanding that neither journey is a mistake.

This time, I listen more,
have more care for others,
welcome and share my sense of home,
and I connect more with my people
as I think of the long line of generations
of the family on this land from the start
to the possible future.

I thank all who have come before me
with such humbleness and gratitude,
and I forgive—
myself first, and where needed,
my family—past, present, and future;

I try to give more, work harder, persist longer,
be more playful, less sensitive to criticism,
laugh more at my follies,

and accept that I am not needed everywhere—

and never was—knowing finally, that others
are most assuredly better suited for debate
and conflict over the use of power than myself—

may our gifts and interests continue without apology.

Along the way, I know,
I do not always get it right,
as I am a sometimes clumsy, unwise,
and imperfect improver and peacemaker,

and though happiness sometimes eludes me,
I am more at peace,

through a more created purposefulness
than ever before; a correlation key
to my branching awareness, that in this life,
though I am still not needed—

by nature's gift, the knowledge gained,
and through others' grace,

here on this land—

the more I care,

the more I cannot be replaced.

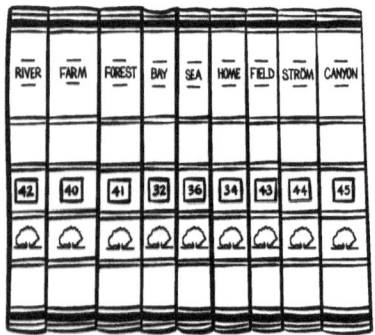

Blue Smoke Around the Card Table

In the time of my youth,
I heard many a rebuke,
on my sensitivity to smoke at my booth.

Were my tears for my card hand,
or the blue air that was fanned?

Certainly, move or be damned.

Around the old, yet lively game table,
a few adults were quite health-loving and stable,
but a few expressively
waived wide their hands through the air
like both a low lit cave torch and a rusted, flaking saber.

Though we now deeply know
that cigarette smoke,
is like inhaling time-released death strokes—
hopefully, in my case, over time,
it is cured by red wine and fun folks.

Strangely, still, sometimes
I even crave the social blue fog of war,
with even negative smell remembrances
deep in mind or on the fore,

smoke covered clothing,
red eyes, yet seemingly for many
it is now just lore.

But, *oh* the good
tear-jerk, raucous laughs
that were had,
somehow make it all
so much bigger than life and not so bad;
like shad on the river,
time makes all things a fad.

As an adult,
what I would not sometimes give and do,
to be back playing again
in that era and hue—
I would have one more day
to see you all through the blue.

Shared Well

Water abounds,
but some soil confounds,
for sandstone gives, and it takes.

So deeply infused with rich, rusted iron,
do not shower long,
if first confused, orange skin is your due.

Sometimes it makes sense
to go over the fence
to share well water of quality,

but beware of the lair,
which comes if you share—
better to write the rules down,

or you might have to face
a lawyer from town,
since clear boundaries make for good families.

And, take note in the summer,
when the water does slumber,
or you might run both the well
and your friendship dry.

Cow Jam

My first word as a child was *cow*.

At five o'clock,
twice each-and-every day,
some fifty-five cows, or more,
would pass my way,

one-hundred yards back from the grey gravel
and manure-spackled country road,
I sometimes looked through
the front house windows
as they slowly passed my parent's abode.

A sound click and a clack,
a quick, sweet-stolen stop
for some fresh grass,

with a hand pat from the farmer
and barks from the dogs,

the cows would almost reflexively splat,
then again return to all musically moving
along to the fields.

My parents told me,
the farmer was needed
with his dogs and his family
to protect those cows
from getting lost on their way
from day-fields to night-hills,
and back again each day.

In return, the cows did relay—
circular-shaped, past-feed
for neighbors to circuitously dodge
on their rounds to town
and milk—the fruit of present and future hay,
which allowed the farmers to be paid.

All, so the farmer, his dogs, and his family
could afford to continue that way of life
to walk those fifty-five, easily-lost-cows,
past my parent's driveway,
at five o'clock,
twice each-and-every day,
seven days a week,
so 365 days per year.

Now older,
whenever I start to feel burned out,
fatigued, irritated by routine,
or not sure where in life I am going,

I often remember that good farmer
with his dogs and his family, and I think:

—*Routine, what am I complaining about?*

There are days too when I am
sitting and looking out my front window
(no longer on the farm)
and a mail carrier passes my way,
at approximately the same time
each-and-every day,
and I immediately think of the cow jam.

I then start feeling nostalgic
as I remember drinking
cows' milk fresh from the dairy,
or hearing cow hooves echoing
with a hollow and soothing click and clack
off the river road through the valley,

and even strangely enough,
the often tedious,
summer afternoon washing
of fresh cow manure off my parent's cars.

Today, when I think back,
I can so easily hear and see
that procession of cows where I grew up,
and the farmer with his dogs,
and his family,
keeping those cows on their way,
and I am grateful.

I think to myself:

I love those farmers—

(click) they helped me find my first word,
(clack) they let me feed the calves bottles,
(click) they let me scoop the grain in the loft,
(clack) and play in the milk barn,
(click) and spend time with them and their animals.

So, my first word was *cow*,

and I finally realize
that the farmer with his dogs
and his family,

kept more than cows
on that country road
from getting lost.

Firewood Row

There is a vast mental row
that each summer I must tow,
since collected firewood for the farm
has yet to stack itself in the barn:

*—Now, lay down the boards,
each row holds a cord,
and they must be level and stable,
but take care of the gaps,
for air must be able to take laps;
can I throw the dog's racquetball
through some of the holes?*

*—Ten cords are a must,
engineered like a truss,
administered in trust,
adherence or bust.*

—I am not sure I have been building so well.

*—This reminds me of my winter of discontent,
when I cared little to remix
the piles I stacked like a 600 brick wall,*

windblown woodpiles faltered and altered,
left uncovered too long to dewater—
some sad woodstove fires that year!

—So, split-faced side down,
make sure the bark side abounds,
nature knows how to help keep its wood dry.

—Tarps, tarps—I must now affix,
more than halfway down is the gist,
for two things I want to accomplish—

keep the wood dry
and do not let the wood fly.

Maybe next year I will just move to town.

Short Rib

I once had a steer,
little more than a year,
which we kept in a small,
and rectangular field in front
of my parent's ranch house.

Good meat he provided friends and family,
or at least that is what they all tell me,

for my attention was often strained
by youths' self-reflection,
the games, and the play.

—*This tastes amazing, Dad!*

—*Oh, you think so?*
—*I'm so glad; I was sorry to let the beef go.*

Perfectly plated at that table
was asparagus, roasted red potatoes, brown rice,
with a medium-rare, lightly seasoned,
and half-eaten steak,
I knew only as my pet steer—
Short Rib.

A long time before I was able to greet,
anything that I thought resembled such meat;
by that hard-cut lesson, I learned—
some types of friendships are burned.

Himalayan Blackberry

Considered a berry,
but really an aggregate fruit,
in short—good to eat,
but hard to treat.
Once cultivated, but now on the run,
a challenge to have a go,
only thorn-slowed by a mow,

so most decide to use
herbicide with a good sticker,
but digging up will also suffice.
Born in the cradle,
with the mind of a ladle,
it made its way
to live free as a wild crop.

Many people value the taste,
but I suspect those who own land,
which Himalayan blackberries embrace,
deep in their soul,
feel a bit more chaste—
for this damn fruit has no limit to growth.

How much over the years has been spent,
on poison poured with no sustained dent?

If more effective options were found,
I could invest the money locally,
in better helping my family and friends,
instead of spraying questionable chemicals
as my maintenance account money goes down
and some corporation's dividend payments go up.

So, what can I do to save the fields?

I hope the answer is not to give up and
buy and hold chemical company mutual funds.
(I am too stubborn and affected, I guess).
I hear Tansy Ragwort is now under control;
can we retrain the underemployed
cinnabar moth, flea beetle, and seed head fly?

The Himalayan blackberry is out of hand—
I will give almost anything new a try to free the land.

Summer Hammocks

Imported, colorfully woven hammocks,
spread over five varied microclimate acres,
with no obstructed views of the river below,

moss-covered old burn piles,
and the broken-down kiln
of an old brickmaker—

I think I shall tarry in this bed in the air,
I believe I will get an answer
to some of my cares,

maybe I will just listen a little longer
to the soft summer breeze
as the tuned tree limbs sing
and rustle the leaves,

for I think I was star born
in a garden for all seasons,
or as close as one can find
for a rascal and work heathen.

They say I am lazy,
no cares in the world,

but I am tuned to a calling
to order what is swirled.

No one can be sure
of how much time they have
to be useful, truthful,
and in periods of great misery
to be a most comforting salve.

Conceivably, not all on my very own,
this inherent, nascent desire to assist
since great books brought me up,
and by modeled duty and loyalty
I learned I can always
look for opportunities
to do more for people in my midst.

Give me a chance to stretch out
in this fine hammock and discover,

I may find kind, rare other world views
so useful to time-sore others.

Like all growing things,
to better cooperate
and sometimes compete—
we all need good soil, healthy air, clean water,
and peace-filled time to be replete.

So many hidden good things I find here,
leisurely lying about—
the abundance of connectedness,
hope, love, and nature's leisurely presence
(and it is not yet noon on this warming Saturday)
confirms for me, this is my route.

Woodstove in the Old Ranch House

In fall, winter, and early spring,
grey plumes of smoke
sometimes twist and wring,
so for fun in the home,

we sit by the stove,
fully embraced and heated
in a peaceful trove.
How many fires, has this home seen?

How many mires, this home gave lean?
A crackle here, a sudden pitch pop, the scent of alder,
all in a shot; many days I have been away,
in my mind's eye, this day I sought.

Oh, give me days of heavy rain,
send me waves of levy wane, so in this place,
I may unhurriedly enjoy a healing, Finnish heat,
a warm reminder of life's kinder feat.

Born in this valley
or come here freight—
know we are gifted now—
let our cares abate.

To Town

Some go every day
to get a sweet treat,
while others hunker way down
as if on retreat;

I tend to think that the type of "riverite" you are
does not matter at all,
since both come from a place
of more privacy and fresh trees that are tall.

They come from a place
not always easy and fair,
so they travel with hardiness,
good instincts, and great care,

since robustness it takes
to live so far from the gates of the town
with a particular steeliness driving straight
along the river road to not drown,

but it is hard to expect
to live there long all alone
when the country calls out
for you to eventually atone,

so connect with your neighbors
and offer a favor,
they will be sure
to do the same for you.

Cookies at holidays,
or mow a little more of the shared road,
drop off some stitching, or a regional,
heartfelt, poetry book ode.

SETTING III
FOREST

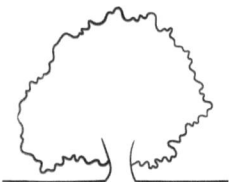

*My dreams they know as their own
as my loves they have watched over,
guided, and welcomed home.*

Through the Canyon to the Clearing

Salt charged air . . . settle down . . .
move through old-barked Douglas fir,
rough western red cedar,
and knobby bigleaf maple—

now move farther in, under the tree canopy—
feel the crisp breath of alder, myrtle, hemlock,
and dew dabbed underbrush
of salmonberry, and fern as a staple.

No other place would I rather be,
then in the base of this canyon encased,
in nature's woody, coarse, and fine debris.

No matter how drawn, city-weary, or sad,
I know this fresh air is the best I have ever had—
so I will breathe in deeply,
as I gently pass through the damp canyon
of yellow-green moss filtered
old-growth timber air.

An inclusive companion as I step softly,
sinking slightly on the duff
of the absorbent forest floor bed of dark brown,
wet-molted, soil-like leaves,
days past branches, fallen plants,
lost flowers and stem greaves.

Through this overgrown dirt cat-logged road
the younger trees have me almost swaying
as I hike to the hilltop of light and good birdsong
on the saddle-shaped road covered in grass,
in an iris-bloomed, seldom traveled tree clearing,
a cozy fifteen feet wide and a peaceful sixty feet long—
one of nature's hammocks—perfect for belaying.

I give a grateful look above
as I walk into the clearing
out from the thick,

swaying arc of a partially locked-arm tree canopy
of mixed, rusting colored, chattering-dry
resigned leaves—as if cheering.

I move away from supported, light-sorting,
thin finger-like branches,
and the penitently and demurring
bent shadows from
tree limbs, old stumps,
long-stretching rhododendrons,
and wild rose thorned stems.

Always such a sudden,
unexpected becoming,
the connecting of nature
from shaded to lighter—
something different and wonderful,
and sorely needed for my soul today,
so in need of repose and spiritual miter.

A Walk Up the Draw to Recharge

Summer so lends to jaunty bends,
and I am called to walk up the draw.

A reverberant call to roam amidst the loam—
every time I feel I am home.

How many have felt the same?

Now running, climbing, jumping, stumping—
here in this moment, life is thumping—
and I feel alive and healthy,
never so wealthy,

for what do I work for if not for this?

What few cares were even brought,
a break shall make for naught,
with my dwindling public awareness;

so, along this course,
I will just keep walking deep
in this creek to find the source.

Here true nature is the feature,
and, privacy the teacher,
may it find me a worthy creature.

I know by heart the refrain,
never fall in love with the farm,
nothing more can be gained,
and it usually will just end in harm.

But, love is not reason,
no matter the season,
and sometimes the land chooses you.

So, I must limit my expenses,
and take care of the fences,
while mending the hives
and harvesting the honey,

which helps me build
multiple increasingly passive revenues
(limited goods they may be),
working toward them is still my life's chosen dues.

All while I pursue
the old path to glory in any age
of working a little good each day
to keep a purpose and in motion,

for the day will surely come,
when my body is undone,
and I will likely have to move away,

so I will sit in this fortuitous moment,
and I shall clearly savor and own it,
knowing heaven on earth,
for me, is in this brief bestowment.

Endless Ferns

Walking clear, mind no fear,
I exalt in one of nature's pronged lungs,
damp earth inhaled down and sung.

Hands wide open by my side,
fern fronds sliding through fingers clawed,
rough between, seeds pop off,
raw spine-felt-jolt, full meaning awed.

Fronds thrown high, low confetti aired,
spread in the soil, for nature's boil.

Returning, exhale from fortunes gate,
a thousand walks will never sate;
no sense of time yet always late.

In the canyons, I sense their strength
pressing, holding, arms stretched out,
like partially buried statues whole and stout—

my audience since I was young,
they have heard my speeches
and accompanied my songs.

My dreams they know as their own
as my loves, they have watched over,
guided, and welcomed home.

When most fatigued,
or when I am about to fall,
I find ferns soft as safety netting
and as perfectly installed—
they always wish me well as I pass by,
out the opening tunnel-shaped canyon,
through the tree-top-clearing sky.

When I Grow Up

In the Coos River Valley, put out your hand
and you are likely to touch a tree,
if you keep your hand on for long,

the advice may come free.
When I was young, I lived in the now,
but by eight, I often wondered about my fate.

On a contemplative walk,
during an afternoon dawdle with life,
I once set the palm of my hand
open touching on an old, woodpecker-holed
and rock-rough to the touch, volunteer pear tree;

suddenly, many professions
flashed through my mind
and it told me all the things
I would *not* grow to be,

which was so strange
that my hand reflexively pulled away,
and I felt stung by a combination
of loss, regret, stinging nettle, and bee—

it was stark and apparent, even as a child,
I experienced something spiritual,
maybe few ever see.

I left the forest sometime later,
with fewer work options
and even more questions;
none more on my mind
than if this all meant I would die young,

or if this tree was saying, more hopefully,
a heart-matched profession
was in the future, yet to be.

As I got a little older, I often reflected back
on my experience with the forest presence of
seemingly potent mystery and knowledge
that gave me for an instant a third eye
to see history without haulage.

Though grateful to have made
it out of childhood alive,
I was still left figuring out my life's big
question: all the remaining things I *would* grow to be.

I was feeling the pull of that twisted vision,
of an intriguing future deep in my being,
but I could see no correlation
to my current actions, for the fruits of gifted
subtractive knowledge, still leave much to see;

I felt this forsakenly, even immaturely,
on my extended amble between
unsatisfying jobs, lost loves, and too much taking
from others while trying to figure life out,

I was never quite wholly free of the day
I came across that old tree, even while walking
in a healing canyon or paddling on a river
to the mountain or the sea.

The weekend before I finally moved
from home, while out cutting a few
dead firewood trees for my parents,

I ventured into that old,
hollow, and slowly departing,
myrtle grove, I never came to alone,
and I finally sought out

that volunteer, long-past pear maker,
seemingly childhood haunter
and planter of seeds of confusion,
over-reflection, and doubt.

It was almost leafless then, punky, yet
surprisingly strong; I angrily raised
my ax to the hollow trunk
to finally be done with it,

but at that moment, I finally felt free,
so I placed my hand palm open upon it,
once again, feeling strangely this time,
that was where it was supposed to be,

and for just an instant, I thought it again spoke to me;
startled and excited, I prepared then and there
to have my future settled
and the full meaning finally gleaned,

yet this time, I sensed no pain,
and when I listened, felt and saw nothing;
only observant nature greeted me.

Now that I am much older, better traveled,
steadily careered, and even bolder,
I still walk the forest
where that old pear tree used to be,
and I wonder—

was that time nothing but a child's-mind,
first self-awareness smolder,
or a sign of something more magical,
and yet to be finished until I am still older.

Myrtle Nuts

Coos River myrtle nuts
so abound and implore,
that I find it funny and quite shocking
that I have so often overlooked and discounted
what is so easily found, perfectly quirky,
and designed to astound and adore.

Am I the only one, or is something bigger at play?

Perhaps the tree's often majestic full grown size
somehow obscures and makes one's mind
not see its myrtle nut commercial potential—
even when it is young,
this old-spirited, uncaught-at-the-root tree
seems to confuse and almost propel us away—

if you cut too close, prepare for a blurring,
almost mystical protective presence
of oil released burning, peppery aroma
and beguiling eye-watering defenses.

Who is the smart one here,
the gatherer, or the tree?

Early to grow after logging, land clearing,
and fire's soil baked heating,
yet last to die, even after the same.

I think dried myrtle nuts taste
most like coffee and dark chocolate,
similarly, mysterious and entreating.

Raw—green, like an undried walnut
the size of a marble,
it tastes strongly astringent and bitter,
like uncured olives or acorns,
a quick bite sends the taster's
smacking lips toward a drink to not wither.

Baked up nicely—enjoyment secured,
though I suspect
few will ever know the taste,
its tree nut existence
still somehow demurred;

since if myrtle has its way—
though adored in some discerning circles
it will always be—it may yet continue
to stay wild, full of guile, and free.

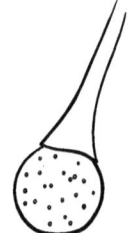

Skunk Cabbage

Skunk cabbage and mud,
oh, what a pair they make,
guilt by association,
this lowly cabbage's reputation cannot break,

but as a gift to the land,
it is quite grand,
and it so much wants
to be giving, comfortable, and liked,
not just a friend prop,
contained and not entertained.

A retiring nature it does possess—
it will never win with the press,
but who cares since it is one of nature's
unassuming hoards,
and what it does to scale
is its own reward.

If human—skunk cabbage is equivalent
to a person who is financially responsible
by hard work and/or good fortune,
but due to material choices

in housing, clothing, and appearance,
is judged by their neighbors
as lacking flair, too frugal,
and beyond the pale,

and *pail*, as a heterograph, is canny
and useful to consider, if stretched,
as well as a sensible analogy to skunk cabbage,
for it even has some leaves,
with a sense of economy, shaped like a trough.

On generally abundant amounts of water, it sits,
on underappreciated marsh-like pits,
not too far from a spring,
well water it may bring,

now, most people get water by drill,
but by doing so how they surely miss
the great triumph of finding such a thrill.

Not only water it shares,
but its roots also have abundant food to bare,
making a fine hidden treat for a spring bear
or as an unassuming life model for a wise heir.

Chittum Bark

To make a few bucks
in spring to early summer
I used to help take my grandfather's truck
to fill the bed high with chittum bark,
and only a pocketknife was often used
to cut from base to the top without an ark.

The pay was not great
for such piecemeal work in the stand,
but all said, I was not so rich
as a child to not give it a hand.

The smell of the bark,
made the knowledge quite stark,
and I was reminded again—
like so many times before—
that making money on a lark
is most often not a walk in the park,

and speaking of a lark,
did its use when applied to fingers
really ever help people
not to bite their fingernails?

As work though, it was better than some activities,
I could have been doing
as I suppose there were a few
people around who were not so honest and true
to make bread by the sweat of their brow—

like who the hell buys chittum bark anyway?

And, who really are these chittum bark dealers working for?

In the end, this was just one false start,
and indeed, financially off the mark,
yet it has become part of the fun youth in my heart.

Maple Leaves Piled in the Dry Creek Bed

Early fall at the canyon forks—
dry, empty creek beds bridged
with maple leaves by the armloads—
the warlike trenches packed with yesterday's sun,
tomorrow's dirt, and the day's energy.

On our bikes, we would hop
off the ramp with a glide-drop,
a soft landing the goal for the day;
ending wet-matted and tattered,
but like the leaves—thoroughly used up, by hard play.

The climb out was a bit of a slippery ascent,
so strong muscles were needed for prolonged reaching
toward snapping roots and short dirt-hold grips,
and it is funny to me that I do not remember
any thoughts about hitting protruding rocks
or a creek's edge;

maybe not surprising
for kids full of unfettered days and no parents near,
with the only real fear being that the day
would go way too quickly
before it was time for big meals of good cheer.

Today, I still get such a bolt,
when the leaves on the trees turn yellow
and they fall to the ground where I live,

though too old now to have a second go,
I offer a smiling embrace
when I think back to those days
so full of all the new seasons' joy
and all the fearless, free-falling flow.

Myrtle Grove

A slippery lot,
leaves beneath the tree knots,
so I try not to slide down the hill.

Thick is the floor,
with nature's galore,
so prolific is this forest duff,
but no matter how many,
always room for more penny-colored leaves.

I wave my hands through blue, greenish-grey moss,
of fine dangling tree reams of time and loss,
a creaking warily sound, a snap may abound,
if the wind picks up in the afternoon.

Dark and clean is the scene,
everywhere in between under the canopy
in this pleasantly covered,
once temple moor, made hollow rune.

Cleanse my worldly cares,
let go of despair,
this place is where I can just be,

for how else to explain,
the release of my pain,
in this shelter from trauma and care.

My journey was long,
here I belong,
as I look at the river through the trees,
seeing birds in the air, showing little care,
as they ride gusty winds
through embracing air pockets
in the sky above me.

This ground has been protected
from most of the evils, I fled,
naïve it is not, as all deep time is fraught;
it too has seen dreams come to naught.

Its first peoples removed
after a too short, spirit-filled,
and symbiotic stay,
and knowing its part in the era,
it still mourns in its own way.

It, too, knows my ancestor's loss and pain
and it shall wash with the rain
only some of our joined hurt, anger,
and remorse away.

Listen, it is calling,
all nature is falling
in rhythm like these heavy,
slow dripping, raindrop-ridden leaves.

So infrequently these days,
I seem to hear anything beyond my next fear,
if only I would, I might get back some
of my energy and genuine desire for health-gains.

So, I breathe deeply
and exhale any need for constant grit,
tense my muscles and release buried stress—
hoping once again my mind will finally return fit;

yet, no need to visualize a relaxing place to be,
for wholeness is the essence of this grove now,
full of silence, presence amending, and home.

Rancher and a Logger

Six foot two, naturally athletic, an original,
with almost nothing he could not do,
this son born of the Oregon Coast Range—

some say touched by its spirit,
a walking embodiment,
a one-person, temporary,
self-learning grange.

Be broken down flat,
or out of sweet diesel or pungent gas,
he would stop to see you were alright,

if you needed help, he was there for you,
not unlike in many ways to Paul Bunyan,
but the stories were true,
and really, a better logger the world never knew.

In younger days,
wild as untamed spring forest power,
everything is a test,
each second, minute, and hour—

wrestle the bull elk,
outswim the salmon,
race and outclimb the black bear,
trick the coyote,
manage the faller,

build the dock,
help the old,
chance and win the games,
raise the cattle,
fix the fences,
and visit the family—

along the way,
drink the coldest beer
and strongest whiskey,
deep smoke,
chew the tinned-tobacco,
but keep the coffee hot.

The walking grange—
knowledge of man breaks upon itself
to see anew the land
has a final fleeting thought.

Smart was the man,
who had the heart of the land
as a rancher and a logger;

when older, known as generous,
tenacious, entertaining, creative,
family-focused, and born an era too late,
so what a loss
with his sudden bidden final rest call,
he, who contributed so much to his kin
with his hard-fought, crest run.

Buried by kinetic tree crown,
held fast by the forest floor,
one last log left on the ground—

where it lay in truce—
see, even the best cannot look up and live
when it is time for the gift to be returned,
the knowledge gained, and spirit loosed.

Some of us seem meant
to be but briefly and brightly lent
as stories to keep in our sphere,

lines shot, corner markers set in nature's-acre,
recorded as country heart-history keystones—

reminding us that when there are few words left to speak,
distance excuses us, and the ties of generations
become weak, we were once bound together
by a binding and renewing source—

caring, improving, and believing that good histories,
are often ours to steadily seek and actively support.

Living Near the Stream

Weather wrought, soil gained,
root was loosened by the rain,
a tree brought down during the night,
the road is open now, but with a fight.

Looks like it is late to work once again
after heading back to the house
to shower and change,
since now a dress shirt and pants,
maybe a blouse,
are covered in—woodchips,
dirt, bar oil, gas, and the rain,

but today, you are the hero neighbor,
the chosen one,
who gets to remember that our river road
is mostly—clean, maintained,
partially paved and graveled,

which just happens to be located
in a coastal mountain range,
with a temperate rainforest climate
full of neighbors the whole way
with occasionally, untimely falling trees.

Oh, one more thing—
for the good deed of
using your very own chainsaw,
so others could drive through,
and you so quickly placed in the back,
of your once clean,
but now dirty—car, truck or SUV,

it *too* is full of sawdust, sticking in a ream,
and will need to be cleaned
as a meditative practice,

I like to call—*living near the stream.*

Froze Last Night

Awake with a quiver,
my body in a shiver,
did it snow so early
in the canyon this fall?

No, just a deep glossy frost,
and the grass is awash
as white as the freshly driven snow,
so I must tramp around,
chores do abound—
oh, how I love to see
my footprints left on the ground.

Like a beautiful old map,
full of dashes like a double-headed crossed ax
(as I look back) this way and that I went,
the ground is a crunch, today at least until lunch—
better tighten my jacket and pull down my warm hat.

This day is for me, and I am so full of glee,
I get to live out in these woods.

Never so sweet is the joy
that comes from the bad which we beat—
escaping the city is grand,
so I will walk up the hill, just for the thrill
to let my breath feed these great trees,

my lungs and these pines
reverse and achieve
a harmony so good for the soul.

Made for each other, this frost will not smoother
but only enhance and bring sight to our kinship,
so for a few more minutes,
let us offer each other our shared gifts as life-holds.

Dusk

Heavy eyes of rods,
more light comes in, slowing now,
the day is dim. Deer wander by,
none I care to keep,

they will make it safe through
tonight's sweet sleep.
The fountain of light has spun away,
evening lulls without delay;
my blessings, pains, and complex thoughts
are invited now to quieter spots.

A comforting form to take to sleep,
candlelit rhyme resounding through blinks.
No matter the outcome, all I can say,
not all were so lucky on this day—
less than a flutter in what is time,
infinite existence or just a line.

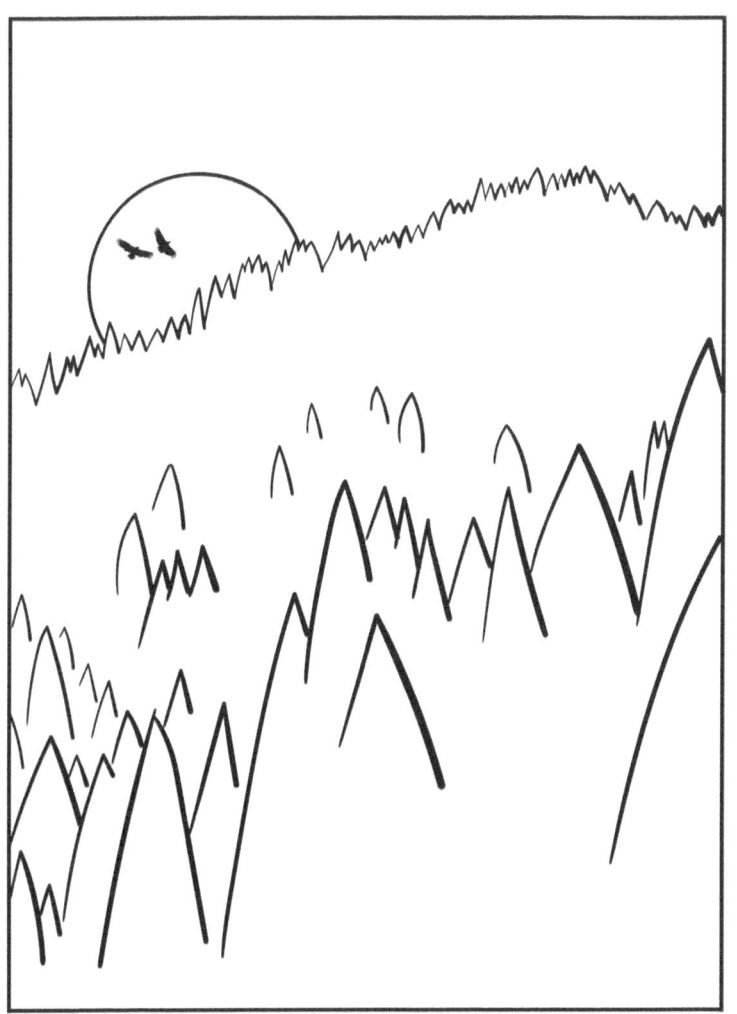

Acknowledgments

Poetry started for me with H. Robert Hamilton, a grandfather figure, who spent many afternoons reading Henry Wadsworth Longfellow, William Shakespeare, Edgar Allen Poe, Robert Frost, Walt Whitman, Emily Dickinson, and many other poets with my brother and me in my childhood.

Thank you (to my lovely wife), Sarah Craig, who is immensely talented and a key supporter of my writing journey these last few years. She is the author of *The Holiday Window Painting Book*. Her MBA from Western Governors University and her Bachelor of Science in Journalism from the University of Oregon, original artwork, and publishing praxis through Thoughts on the Good Life Press made it possible for this second collection of poems to find its way out into the world.

Thank you, Shelly Krehbiel, whose Master of Fine Arts in Creative Writing from Antioch University and skill in poetry, provided me with essential developmental editing at an important time in the project.

I would also like to thank my parents, Lorenzo and Laura Craig, and my brother, Jason Craig, for their technical advice on several poem concepts regarding building, cooking, labor, and recreational activities for general accuracy.

Excellent technical support and lessons for both Adobe InDesign and Adobe Illustrator, related to cover design, page layout, and graphic design were provided by the team of Angle Daschel and Adam Rolison of BrickAndBalloon.com.

Paintings on page 76 and 98 were painted by the talented Portland, Oregon artist Joan Frazer in 2016 (Summer Home) and 2014 (Ranch House). My appreciation to Meghan (Major) Stark for taking a picture of the Coos River, used on page 30.

"Looking Out the Classroom Window," and "Late Fall in the Work Fields," had final stanzas inspired by specific ideas in the books: *Cradle to Cradle* and *Every Family's Business*, respectively.

In addition to those already mentioned, many other individuals helped with particular aspects of the review or creative process:

A heartfelt thank you to—Vonnie (Smith) Major; Dennis and Katie Simpson; Richard and Cindy (Craig) Finlayson; Laurie Craig; Steven and Blake Finlayson; Tara (Clarke) MacSween; Julia (Matejka) McMorran; The Craig Group; Carson Craig; Barbara Kanz; Kerry and Josie Finsand; Thomas and Tyan Horn; Jordan and Clare Baskerville; Ryan and Lindsey Weehunt; Jeff and Corrie Davidson; Jordan and Becca Carter; Gary and Lisa Roberts; As well as other individuals, I may have inadvertently missed, if so—*thank you.*

My uncle, Bro Craig, late author of *The Letters*, 2012, who relayed a powerful sense of place, in his novel, set in the Coos River Valley, helped inspire me to start writing again.

Last but not least, I would like to acknowledge the essential work of late author, Charlotte L. Mahaffy, for writing *Coos River Echoes: A Story of the Coos River Valley*, who told a story of the Coos River Valley, which broadly set the stage for this collection of poetry. I believe in many ways, through *Coos River Echoes*, the unique way of life of the Coos River Valley lives on to this day.

Afterword

Near the end of the 19th century, two of my ancestor lines moved to the Coos River Valley. One of which came to the area as part of the Great Migration of Finns into North America; for them, via Korsnäs, Finland, part of the Ostrobothnia region. They spoke Swedish, and the Coos Bay area had a large (for its day) community of Swedish-Finn immigrants. I believe a lot of the mysticism, loss of home, food-related elements, community spirit, and work ethic inspired poems were influenced by the family stories I grew up with. My family still lives on the property, so there is a straight line to the past through the land; I hope it improved this work.

I would also like to recognize that these poems are an incomplete story of the Coos River Valley. This collection is a limited impression and expression of artistic ideas and feelings portrayed over an approximately 150 year time period, based loosely on the concept of one family's thoughts, somewhat overlapping, over multiple generations.

In no way are any of the poems a replacement for historical texts on the area. For example, the Native American experience in the late 19th and early 20th centuries are only lightly covered as they intersected with poems in this work. See the suggestions for further reading to learn more about that era and history.

The book *Coos River Echoes: A Story of the Coos River Valley* can be somewhat difficult to find, so a great way to access it is through a library.

Suggestions for Further Reading

Mahaffy, Charlotte L. 1965. *Coos River Echoes; a Story of the Coos River Valley,*. Portland, Or., Interstate Press.

Craig, Bro. 2012. *The Letters*. La Jolla, CA: Bro III Publishing Co.

Douthit, Nathan. 2005. *The Coos Bay Region, 1890-1944: Life on a Coastal Frontier*. Coos Bay, Or.: Coos Bay Historical Society.

Marlantes, Karl. 2019. *Deep River*. Atlantic.

Collins, Billy. 2012. *The Trouble with Poetry and Other Poems*. London: Picador.

Mortimer Jerome Adler, and Max Weismann. 2000. *How to Think about the Great Ideas: From the Great Books of Western Civilization*. Chicago, Ill.: Open Court.

Mcarthur, Lewis A, and Lewis L Mcarthur. 2003. *Oregon Geographic Names*. Portland: Oregon Historical Society Press; Seattle.

Hathaway Jones, Stephen Dow Beckham, and Christina Romano. 1990. *Tall Tales from Rogue River: The Yarns of Hathaway Jones*. Corvallis, Or Oregon State University Press.

Orvil Dodge. 1969. *Pioneer History of Coos and Curry Counties*, Oregon. Bandon, Oregon: Western World.

Lark, Gary. 2016. *River of Solace.* Oregon: Flowstone Press.

Mcgriff, Michael. 2012. *Home Burial*. Port Townsend, Wash.: Copper Canyon Press.

Youst, Lionel, Ondine Eaton, Sharren Dalke, and Simon Bolivar Cathcart. 2011. Lost in Coos: *"Heroic Deeds and Thrilling Adventures" of Searches and Rescues on Coos River, Coos County, Oregon, 1871 to 2000.* Allegany, Or.: Golden Falls Publishing.

"History – Confederated Tribes of Coos, Lower Umpqua and Siuslaw Indians." n.d. Accessed December 19, 2020. https://ctclusi.org/history/.

"A Changing World – Coquille Indian Tribe." n.d. Accessed December 19, 2020. http://www.coquilletribe.org/?page_id=49.

Stanley, Thomas J. 1996. *The Millionaire Next Door.* New York.

Silverstein, Shel. 1974. *Where the Sidewalk Ends: The Poems and Drawings of Shel Silverstein.* New York, Ny: Harpercollins Publishers.

Thomas William Deans. 2008. *Every Family's Business: A Blueprint for Protecting Family Business Wealth.* Orangeville, Ont.: Détente Financial Corp.

Braungart, Michael, and William Mcdonough. 2002. *Cradle to Cradle: Remaking the Way We Make Things.* London Vintage.

Cunningham, Lillian. "Billy Collins on Life, Death and Poetry." The Washington Post. April 23, 2019. Accessed January 28, 2021. https://www.washingtonpost.com/news/on-leadership/wp/2014/10/03/billy-collins-on-life-death-and-poetry/.

Kahn, Lloyd, Bob Easton, and Shelter Publications. 2013. *Shelter.* Bolinas, Calif.: Shelter Publications.

GUY CRAIG is from Coos Bay, Oregon, where he grew up along the South Fork Coos River. He lives in Tigard, Oregon, and he spends most of his free time in the Coos River Valley.

He holds a Master of Science in Special Education from the University of Oregon and a Bachelor of Science in Psychology from Portland State University. Guy is the author of three other poetry collections: *Idling Intuitions: Poems* (2021); *Amble* (2021), *Mast Years: Poems* (2022). *Coos River Reverberations: Poems of River, Farm & Forest* is his debut book of poetry.

www.ingramcontent.com/pod-product-compliance
Lightning Source LLC
Chambersburg PA
CBHW021108080526
44587CB00010B/442